THIS BOOK BELONGS TO

_____

ISBN: 978-0-9945595-2-4

THE ULTIMATE
AUSSIE FAMILY
ROAD TRIP BOOK

Amy Curran

FOREWARD

Travelling with your kids shouldn't be something that you dread. There are so many ways to make it fun for them, and save your own sanity at the same time.

My own family travels every few weeks, for and trips each way can last up to four hours. I was racking my brain, trying to think of things they could do along the way. We have a DVD player in the car, but honestly, how frustrating is it to have to stop to press play on the Menu screen, or worse, search the car frantically for a disc without scratches!

In this book, you will find lots to keep their minds going, and hopefully stop the "are we there yet's?" There are activities they can do alone, games the whole family can join in, as well as a parents section at the back with some extra ideas.

All your children need is their pencilcase with some pencils or crayons.

I hope you enjoy this book as much as I enjoyed creating it for you.

Amy.

CONTENTS

I ♥ THE ROAD

PLAY
WITH THE FAMILY

Spotto

The aim of this game… everyone looks for the same item and whoever sees it first yells "Spotto". Keep a tally to determine the winner at the end of the drive.

The game is typically played using a yellow car as the object, but for variation, objects could include: personalised number plates, makes of cars, other car colours, etc.

LIFE IS A HIGHWAY

Tic Tac Toe

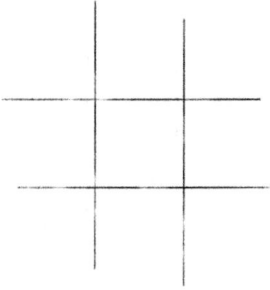 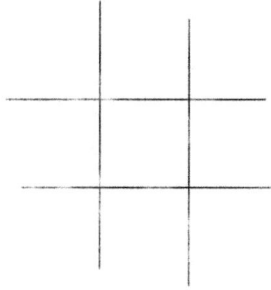 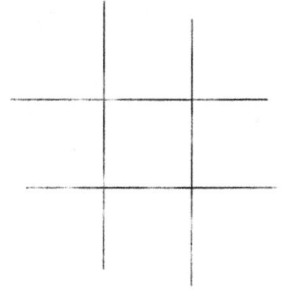

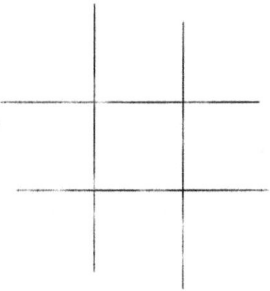 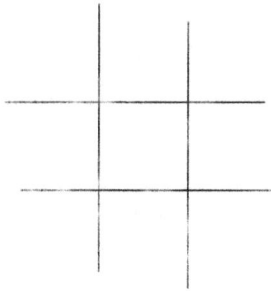 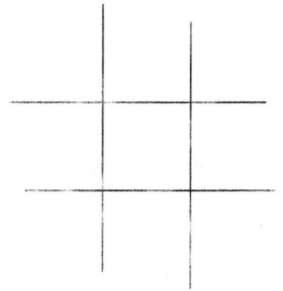

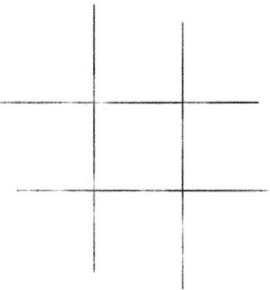 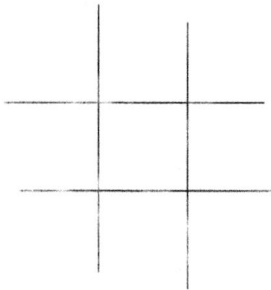 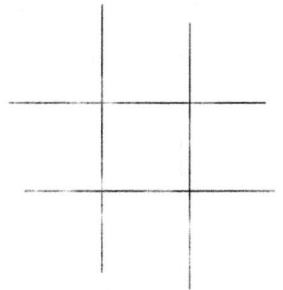

Tic Tac Toe

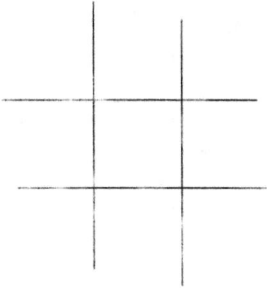
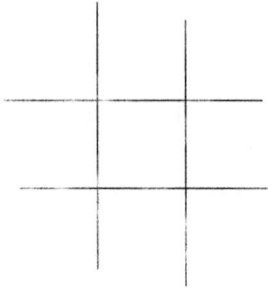
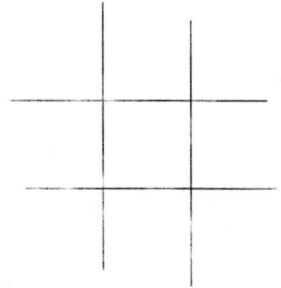
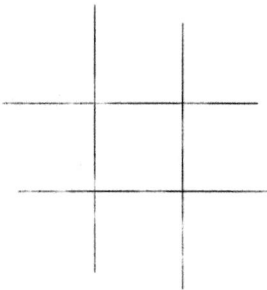
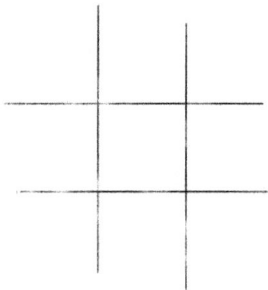
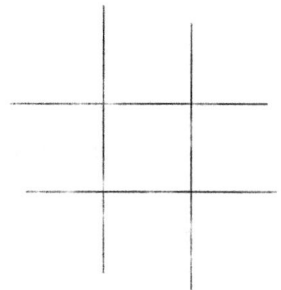
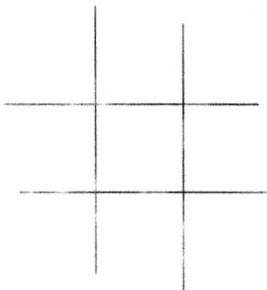
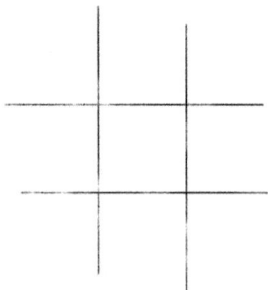
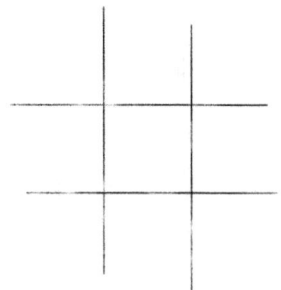

Tic Tac Toe

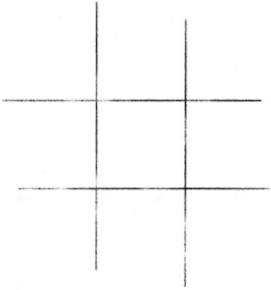 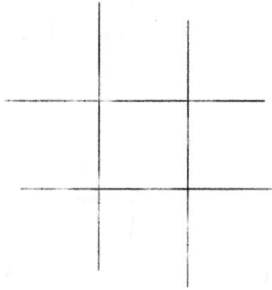 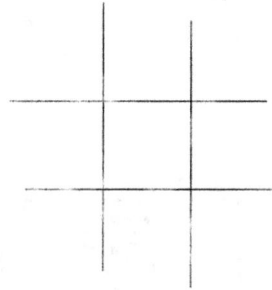

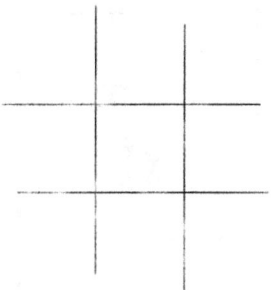 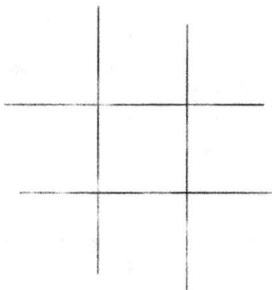 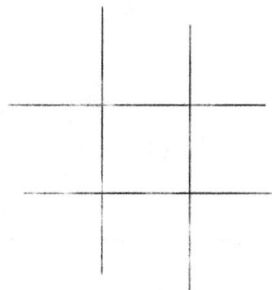

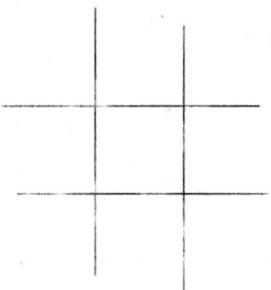 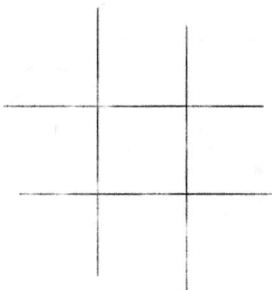 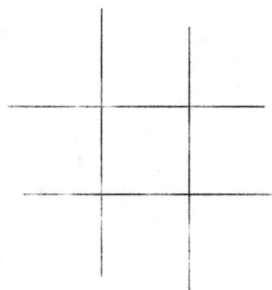

BINGO

As you are travelling, mark off any objects that you see. The first person to get 4 in a row (up, down or diagonally) shouts "BINGO" and is the winner!

Hangman

The first player thinks of a word (a person, place, animal...) and then draws a space for each letter in the word. The second player guesses one letter at a time. If the mystery word/s contain the letter, player one writes it in the correct place. If not, the other player draws a head on the hangman scaffold and continues to draw parts of that body for each wrong letter guessed.

When enough incorrect letters (10) have been guessed, the body is complete and the second player loses. If the guesser solves the puzzle before the body is complete, he wins. You can cross the letters off as you go, so you know what letters you have already guessed.

A B C D E F G H I J K L M N O P Q R S T U V W X Y Z

Hangman

ABCDEFGHIJKLMNOPQRSTUVWXYZ

ABCDEFGHIJKLMNOPQRSTUVWXYZ

Hangman

ABCDEFGHIJKLMNOPQRSTUVWXYZ

ABCDEFGHIJKLMNOPQRSTUVWXYZ

Hangman

ABCDEFGHIJKLMNOPQRSTUVWXYZ

ABCDEFGHIJKLMNOPQRSTUVWXYZ

Dots & Boxes

Each player has their own colour of pen or pencil. Take turns joining two horizontally or vertically adjacent dots by a line. A player that completes the fourth side of a square (a box) colours in that box and plays again. When all boxes have been coloured in, the game ends and the player who has coloured the most boxes wins.

 # Dots & Boxes

Dots & Boxes

Battle Vehicles

A variation on the popular game, 'Battleships', the goal is to find all of your opponents vehicles.

How to play:
Give each player a pencil and one of the grid sheets. The top grid is for your own fleet and the bottom grid is where you try to locate the other player's fleet.

First you decide where to place your own fleet within your grid. Each type of vehicle in your fleet covers a different number of boxes in the grid, as shown, and is drawn vertically or horizontally (not diagonally). Vehicles cannot occupy the same square.

To place a vehicle, check how many boxes are covered by the vehicle and then write the first letter of the name of the vehicle in the boxes it covers. For example, a Car covers two boxes so you would pick any two adjacent boxes and put the letter C in each box. Keep your fleet location secret from your opponent! When each player has marked their fleet on their grid, begin play.

Take turns to find your opponents fleet by calling out the number of a certain box by its grid location. For example, you could call out "B6" or "F1". Your opponent must say whether the shot is a "miss" or a "hit", and, if it is a "hit", what type of vehicle it is. You can keep track of what you have shot on your lower grid, and the vehicles you have found by crossing off the names.

Play continues until one player wins by successfully finding the whole of the other player's fleet.

Battle Vehicles

YOUR VEHICLES

	1	2	3	4	5	6	7	8	9	10
A										
B										
C										
D										
E										
F										
G										
H										
I										
J										

ROADTRAIN (5 spaces)   RRRRR
SEMITRAILER (4 spaces) SSSS
BUS (3 spaces)   BBB
CAR (2 spaces)   CC
MOTORBIKE (1 space)   M

OPPONENTS VEHICLES

	1	2	3	4	5	6	7	8	9	10
A										
B										
C										
D										
E										
F										
G										
H										
I										
J										

Battle Vehicles

YOUR VEHICLES

	1	2	3	4	5	6	7	8	9	10
A										
B										
C										
D										
E										
F										
G										
H										
I										
J										

ROADTRAIN (5 spaces)   RRRRR
SEMITRAILER (4 spaces)   SSSS
BUS (3 spaces)   BBB
CAR (2 spaces)   CC
MOTORBIKE (1 space)   M

OPPONENTS VEHICLES

	1	2	3	4	5	6	7	8	9	10
A										
B										
C										
D										
E										
F										
G										
H										
I										
J										

Battle Vehicles

YOUR VEHICLES

ROADTRAIN (5 spaces)   RRRRR
SEMITRAILER (4 spaces) SSSS
BUS (3 spaces)   BBB
CAR (2 spaces)   CC
MOTORBIKE (1 space)   M

	1	2	3	4	5	6	7	8	9	10
A										
B										
C										
D										
E										
F										
G										
H										
I										
J										

OPPONENTS VEHICLES

	1	2	3	4	5	6	7	8	9	10
A										
B										
C										
D										
E										
F										
G										
H										
I										
J										

BINGO

As you are travelling, mark off any road signs that you see. The first person to get 4 in a row (up, down or diagonally) shouts "BINGO" and is the winner!

STOP	GIVE WAY	LEFT LANE MUST TURN LEFT	(railway crossing T-junction sign)
(pedestrian crossing sign)	(no U-turn sign)	GRAVEL ROAD	SCHOOL ZONE 40 7.30-9AM 2-3.30PM SCHOOL DAYS
ONLY	(roundabout sign)	WRONG WAY GO BACK	GIVE WAY TO STOCK
NO STOPPING OR TURNING	(slippery road sign)	TURN LEFT AT ANY TIME WITH CARE	(kangaroo sign)

DRAWING
& COLOURING

End of the Road

What's at the end of the road? Complete the drawing.

Colour In

Build a Town

Where would you like to go? If you could create your own town to visit, what would it look like? Would there be paddocks, or creeks, or parks... or even a waterslide?

Welcome to

End of the Road

What's at the end of the road? Complete the drawing.

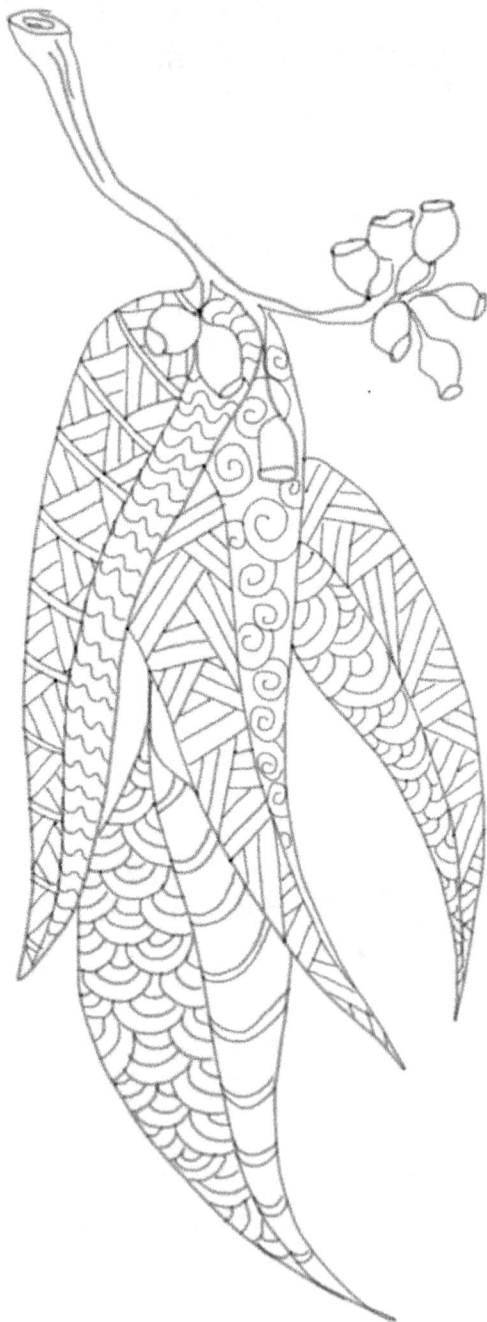

Colour In

End of the Road

What's at the end of the road? Complete the drawing.

What's in the Truck?

What's in this truck? Complete the drawing with what you think would be in the truck.

Colour In

What's in the Truck?

What sort of things are in this garbage truck? Complete the drawing with what you think people may have left out for the garbage man.

PUZZLES
& MAZES

Word Search

Find all of the names of the Animals, Reptiles and Birds that you may see in Australia.

A	H	L	T	J	Z	D	B	Y	B	E	G	B	Q	R
K	R	E	I	C	U	Q	C	S	F	G	A	P	Y	K
F	S	N	A	K	E	D	E	M	Z	E	S	S	P	O
P	Y	B	M	P	V	A	D	L	H	C	O	D	U	O
L	G	O	O	L	L	R	X	K	N	K	W	C	S	K
A	O	G	N	F	A	W	J	Y	P	O	A	J	I	A
T	B	A	T	Z	X	H	V	L	O	I	L	H	K	B
Y	U	M	I	N	A	U	M	R	S	T	L	S	B	U
P	Q	L	W	L	O	Y	A	X	S	E	A	D	A	R
U	Z	S	A	P	A	G	W	I	U	A	B	G	C	R
S	R	G	K	N	N	S	K	J	M	F	Y	H	E	A
T	U	O	N	A	V	Y	L	L	A	N	N	C	K	O
T	O	A	K	O	A	L	A	J	I	A	K	E	C	Q
K	O	L	V	R	R	L	Z	O	G	H	B	P	D	F
G	U	X	M	M	N	W	K	W	O	M	B	A	T	R

KANGAROO	WALLABY	WOMBAT
POSSUM	GECKO	SNAKE
KOALA	KOOKABURRA	GOANNA
LIZARD	GALAH	PLATYPUS

Maze

Find your way through the maze

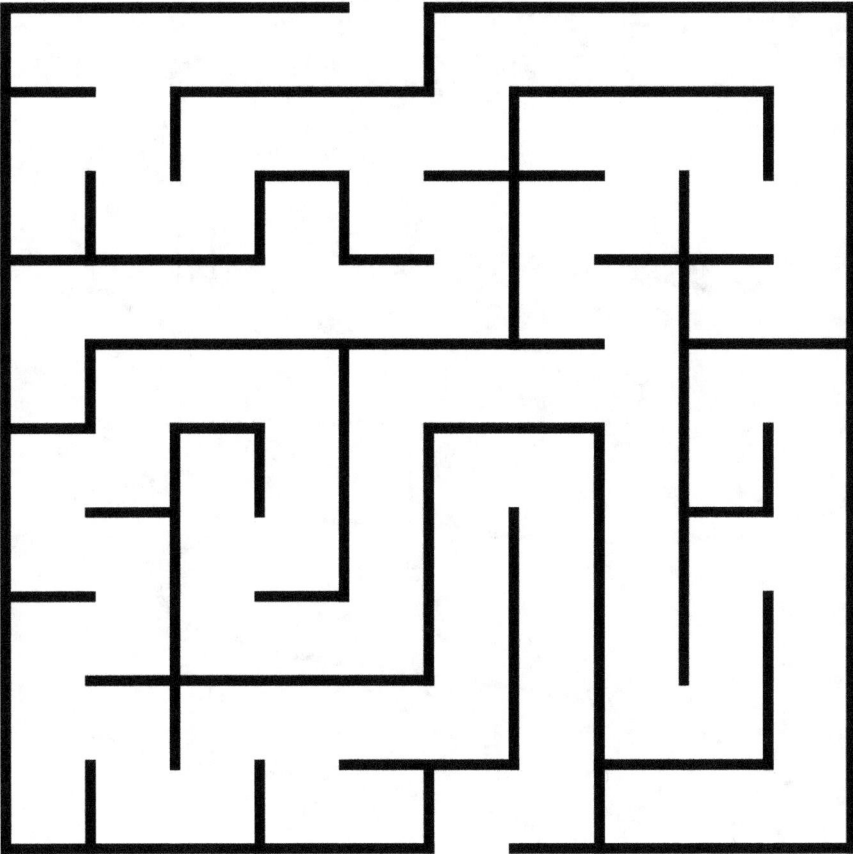

Road Sign ABC

Find these letters on road signs as you drive along. Cross off all of the letters in the alphabet, in order, to reach your destination.

Z Y X W V
Q R S T U
P
O N M L K J
D E F G H I
C B A

Aussie Crossword

Complete the crossword using the clues below.

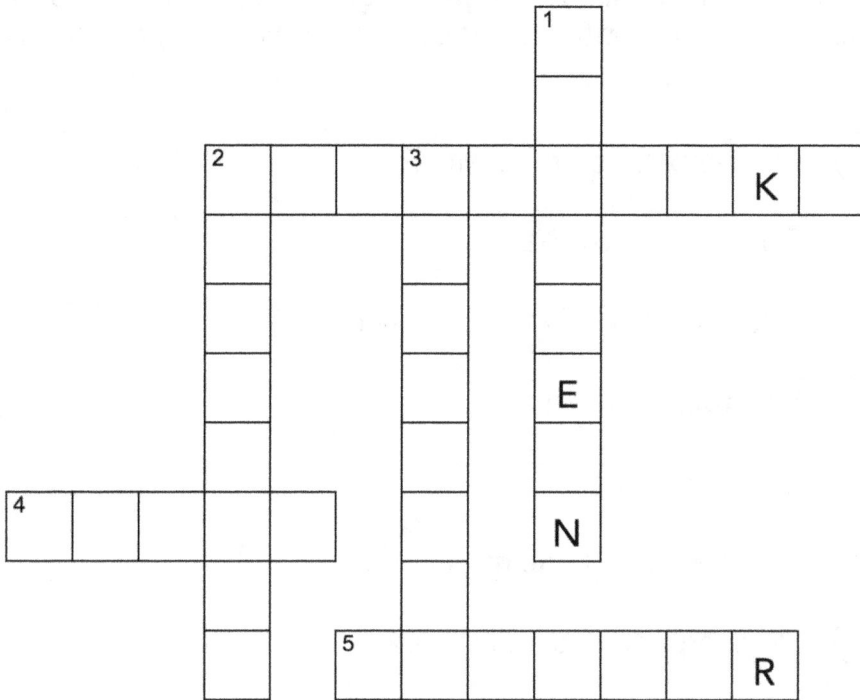

Across:
2. The highest mountain on mainland Australia
4. Ayers Rock also called _____
5. The Great _____ Reef is a National icon

Down:
1. Australia is located in the _____ hemisphere
2. A _____ and an emu are on the National Emblem
3. The capital city of Australia

Scavenger Hunt

See the world around you, look out the windows and mark off all of the items in your Scavenger Hunt.

You can also make this a multi-player game by racing against family member/s in the car with you, and being the first to find them all.

- ◯ Numberplate starting with P
- ◯ Driver wearing a hat
- ◯ Stick figure family window sticker
- ◯ Bike rack on a car
- ◯ Convertible car
- ◯ Two people on one motorbike
- ◯ Numberplate ending with a 4
- ◯ Purple Car
- ◯ Driver or passenger picking their nose
- ◯ Cloud shaped like an animal
- ◯ A truck carrying cars

Word Search

Find all of the names of the Australian Landmarks, Icons and places to see.

A	K	O	S	C	I	U	S	Z	K	O	P	G	A	K
I	S	L	H	T	W	F	S	Y	O	D	Y	D	T	O
O	J	B	R	N	G	E	A	C	V	X	E	F	S	S
K	I	H	M	Q	L	B	F	D	U	K	L	A	B	C
O	P	N	Q	T	K	A	K	A	D	U	E	Y	V	I
P	M	R	S	R	Z	E	J	I	A	Z	G	R	C	U
E	S	O	A	J	K	D	V	N	Y	H	G	E	U	S
R	P	H	T	C	U	L	W	T	F	F	Q	S	H	G
A	S	N	D	B	M	E	J	R	A	X	R	R	V	I
H	G	R	E	A	T	O	C	E	A	N	R	O	A	D
O	K	O	S	B	C	I	W	E	S	E	X	C	C	W
U	X	L	E	P	Z	U	D	A	T	D	B	K	B	R
S	M	C	R	A	D	L	E	M	T	P	A	Q	Y	F
E	O	Y	T	H	R	E	E	S	I	S	T	E	R	S
N	H	A	R	B	O	U	R	B	R	I	D	G	E	Z

AYRES ROCK
OPERA HOUSE
DESERT
GREAT OCEAN ROAD

THREE SISTERS
HARBOUR BRIDGE
KAKADU
SHARK BAY

APOSTLES
CRADLE MT
DAINTREE
KOSCIUSZKO

Maze

Find your way through the maze

Animal Crossword

Complete the crossword using the clues below.

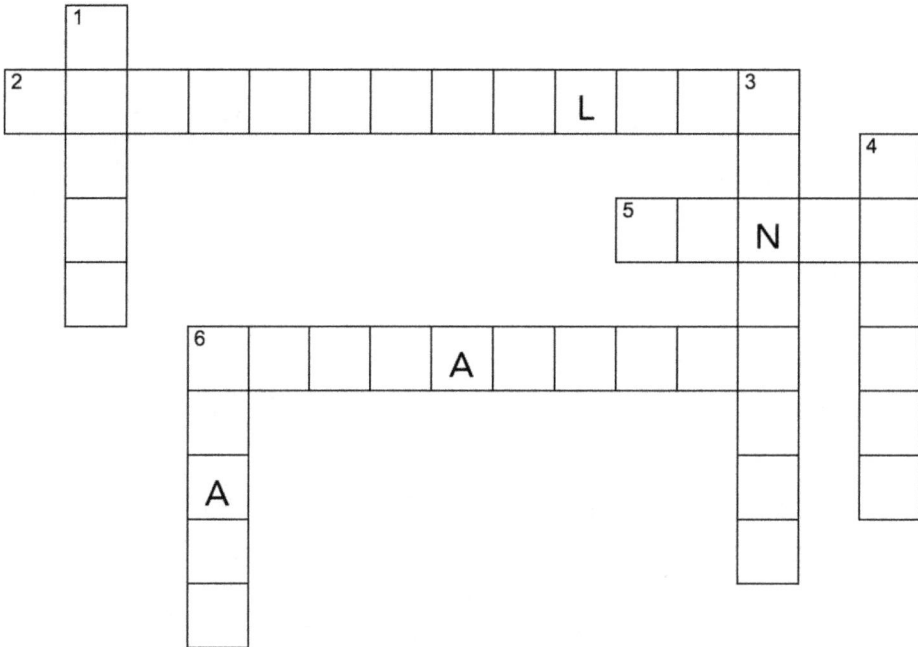

Across:
2. This snake has a coloured underside
5. Native to Australia, but looks very similar to a dog
6. Known for its entertaining 'laugh' like sound

Down:
1. Living in Tasmania, this one is little and scary-looking
3. This animal has a pouch, large feet and 'hops'
4. Round and furry and lives in a burrow
6. Eats gum leaves and is often mistaken for a bear

Spot the Difference

There are 6 differences between these two pictures. Can you find them? Circle them when you do!

Word Search

Find all of the names of the Australian Native Flora.

A	D	M	G	N	M	E	L	A	L	E	U	C	A	E
U	R	O	O	H	C	O	D	S	T	F	B	O	R	O
P	B	W	A	R	A	T	A	H	W	F	L	L	X	Z
G	I	L	Y	P	T	R	S	V	L	E	U	G	M	W
R	Q	B	U	S	H	U	T	E	I	B	W	L	H	A
E	B	T	T	C	B	K	E	U	C	A	L	Y	P	T
V	J	S	L	T	P	A	W	S	P	N	J	D	J	T
I	W	K	N	B	I	Y	R	O	C	K	K	A	I	L
L	P	I	T	T	O	Q	O	L	A	S	G	I	H	E
L	M	P	U	A	H	R	I	Y	C	I	D	S	A	N
E	N	E	O	B	A	C	O	P	Q	A	E	I	C	I
A	L	D	O	G	K	A	J	N	V	M	B	E	F	A
Y	X	N	N	L	E	L	F	S	I	E	S	S	L	L
P	Y	A	Z	M	A	U	K	A	C	A	C	I	A	G
T	K	A	N	G	A	R	O	O	A	W	E	N	D	H

ACACIA	GREVILLEA	DAISIES
BANKSIA	BORONIA	MELALEUCA
WATTLE	KANGAROO PAW	WARATAH
MINT BUSH	HAKEA	EUCALYPT

Maze

Find your way through the maze

Spot the Difference

There are 10 differences between these two pictures. Can you find them? Circle them when you do!

Word Search

One for the Mums and Dads, find the names of Australian Actors, Bands and Musicians.

```
D K Q G Y H J F E E M H O U S E A F E
M I R L P K X I T J K K L E D I G H C
S D E P M A N T E I S H S J C O B O L
T M Q F N O E U D L L U G E R N R Q E
W A T S W H G W Y E O K A C D C O P D
R N R U C E C N Z H I M L Y Z G U E G
V X S N E V I V D N M A N N E F G L E
W E A D U V W E K I D O M D N Y I I R
U L C T I S D Y L S S M I K J O H J X
B S O D X W A B B M M L N I T U L E D
R D L T O V I H A M A N O H C A V W E
Q P D R U O G I R P N A G B A M D C W
C P C D E E L M N D C I U O P I B R U
Q O H A N L X S E P N N E C L Q S O T
N B I M I D U N S D Q X J K C M R W C
R S S W B L A N I O Y S Z B G U E E U
E U E F V Q X M M I L A I Y O U O D B
A M L T L W N Y Z X G H C R O W A T V
C R O C D U N D E E K F G J H R S F E
```

WILLIAMSON	COLD CHISEL	INXS
ACDC	BLANCHETTE	BARNES
LEDGER	CROWE	MINOGUE
KIDMAN	CROC DUNDEE	CROWDED HOUSE
MIDNIGHT OIL	DIVINYLS	YOUAMI

Bumpers

Draw a line as quickly as you can through the road, dodging and avoiding all of the obstacles! Don't crash!

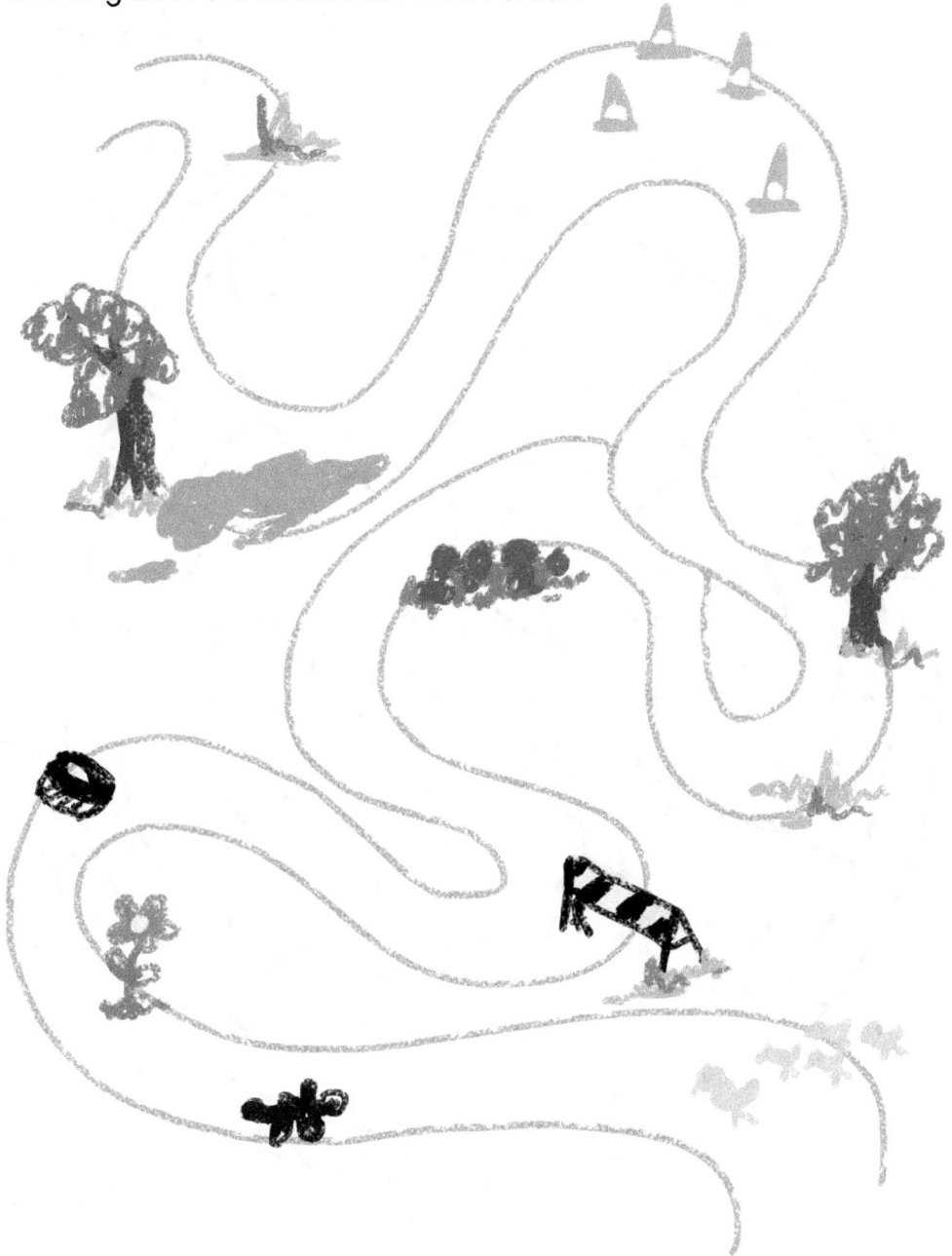

Round Maze

Find your way through the maze

START A CONVERSATION

Would you rather?

Find out the real chacracter of your family members by putting these questions out in the car... take turns being the one who asks the question. Answering 'both' or 'neither' is not allowed. Respond to answers with 'why?' for some extra entertainment!

Would you rather be without elbows or be without knees?

Would you rather wear a snow suit in the desert or be naked in Antarctica?

Would you rather have cookies or have French fries?

Would you rather be super fast or super strong?

Would you rather be invisible or have the ability to fly?

Would you rather eat your boogers or lick your shoe?

Would you rather be a police officer or be a firefighter?

Would you rather be rich and ugly, or poor and pretty?

Would you rather have to fight a Dragon or wrestle an Octopus?

Would you rather be a window or a door?

Would you rather be a kid your whole life, or an adult your whole life?

Would you rather be able to fly, or be able to read minds?

Would you rather be a dog or a cat?

Tell a Story

What better time to engage in a game of group storytelling than when you're captive in a car with your family on a road trip?

There are really no rules to this storytelling game. Instead, it's all about using your creativity to create characters and place them in unexpected situations. One person might start off with, "There once lived a gorgeous girl called Gertie." The next player then picks up the story, adding "She lived in a garbage can behind the school." A third player throws a spanner into the works, adding, "Well, it looked like a garbage can, but really, it was a... "

Adventure Awaits

Twenty Questions

The game can be played by anyone, anywhere and doesn't require any special items to play. The skill level is easily adjusted to any age, as it is only as hard as the actual object is to guess.

The game starts with one player thinking of an object. Then the other players ask questions that can be answered with a "yes" or "no" in an attempt to identify the object. In total the players are allowed to ask a total of twenty questions.

The game is won if a player correctly guesses the object. Then it becomes their turn to choose the next object, and the game continues.

If the players cannot guess the object correctly within the twenty questions the object chooser reveals the answer and gets to choose another object.

Rhubarb

Choose a player to go first. The rest of the players take turns to ask this person questions. The chosen player can only answer "Rhubarb" to these questions.

Questions like... "what do you sleep inside at night?" rhubarb. "what do you clean your teeth with?" rhubarb. "who do you love?" rhubarb.

Player is 'out' if they smile or laugh! Time each go and the one who lasts the longest is the winner.

You can mix it up by letting the winner choose the next word, here are some good ones - Banana, Sausage, Cheese!

IT'S ALL THE LITTLE MOMENTS THAT MAKE LIFE A BIG ADVENTURE

FOR THE PARENTS

Be Road Trip Ready

Get your vehicle road trip ready! Here are some tips to make your journey more comfortable:

1. Give your car a really good clean out. Sounds obvious, but I mean a really good clean out. Glovebox, under seats, etc.

2. Activities for the Kids - Put this book in your car! Along with a loaded pencil case.

3. Stock your glove box with some napkins or wipes for those quick spill clean ups.

4. Don't forget a few plastic bags for rubbish.

5. Look after the car, give yourself plenty of time for this one, in case you need to do any of these points... check:
 - the Tyres... how is the pressure and the tread on each tyre?
 - Wiper blades – The sun can degrade wiper blades fast. If you haven't used your wipers in a while it's a good idea to take a look at them and flip them on to make sure they are running smoothly without making that horrible scraping noise. (While you are there, make sure your wiper fluid is topped off too.)
 - Oil... when is your car next due for an oil change? Even if it is coming up in the future, consider changing your oil before your big trip, the extra road trip kilometres could put you in need of an oil change sooner than usual.

They are just quick things you can check yourself. It is always best to have a mechanic give your car a look over before any substantial trip.

Travel Surprise Bags

Take away some of the "are we there yet" and give the kids some surprises to look forward to along the way.

The bags can be given out any time that suits you and the length of your journey. It can be every 15 minutes, when boredom sets in, or as milestones... eg "Open when we get to Jindabyne".

What you will need:
Brown paper bags
Things to put in them!

Cheap shops are a great place to get supplies. Look for small items like notepads, hand held puzzles, small animal toys or costume jewellery. Anything that your child/ren would usually like.

You can also add some travel friendly treats, like lollipops, to the bags.

Make your own jokes! Write out some jokes and riddles, and add them to the bags.

do not open
COWRA

Packing Tips

1. Know the weather of the place/s you are visiting. This will reduce overpacking significantly.

2. Know the activities you will be doing so you can pack appropriately. You don't want to get to a hiking trip without your joggers and some tracksuit pants.

3. Know the types of accommodation you will be staying at. If you are staying in hotels you won't need to take things like towels or linen. If you are staying in a cabin at a caravan park, then you may need to pack these. Always check.

4. Take less and wash more. You only need one jacket per person, and 2 of each other item.

5. Have a 'travel box' of handy household items that you will need. Things like dishwashing detergent, paper towel, laundry liquid, pegs, bandaids, a torch and toilet paper. Also have a non-perishable box of frequently used food items: salt, pepper, sauce and cooking oil. These are handy whether camping or staying at accomodation, as usually they are not provided.

Travel Snacks

Here are some quick and easy alternatives to 'servo snacks' you can prepare yourself.

KID-APPROVED ROADIE MIX
  1/3 cup Cereal (Fruit Loops, Nutri-Grain or Cheerios are great)
  1/3 cup M&Ms
  1/3 cup Marshmallows
  1/3 cup Sultanas
Mix together gently with hands. Pack in sealed plastic lunch bags, or travel containers.

VEGIE STICKS
Slice carrots and celery into long sticks. You can even add a little tub of peanut butter or cream cheese if they like to dip.

CHEESE AND CRACKERS
Cut up some cheese, and add to plastic lunch bags with different types of cheese crackers.

ICE CREAM CONE CAKES
The day before you go, cook up some cupcakes. Instead of using cupcake wrappers, use flat bottomed ice cream cones. These are surprisingly mess-free, kids will eat the whole lot and you won't be finding cupcake wrappers a week later.

A good mix of healthy and not-as-healthy options are good, kids will be more likely to eat if there is a balance.

Basic Checklist

Mum/Dad
Shorts
Tops
Pyjamas
Jacket
Jeans/Pants
Dress/Skirts
Joggers/Sandals
Dressy Shoes
Underwear/Socks
Swimsuit
Jewellery
Sunglasses

The Kids
Shorts
Tops
Pyjamas
Jacket
Jeans/Pants
Dress/Skirts
Joggers/Sandals
Dressy Shoes
Underwear/Socks
Swimsuit
Favourite Toy/Book
Pencilcase

Baby
Nappies/Wipes
Dummy
Bottles
Formula
Toys
Blankets/Wraps
Suits
Jacket
Footwear/Socks
Monitor
Bathing

Toiletries
Toothbrushes
Toothpaste
Soap/Body Wash
Bubble bath
Shampoo/Conditioner
Deoderant
Razors/Shaving
Hairbrush/Hairties

Handy items
Dishwashing detergent
Paper towel
Laundry liquid/Pegs
Bandaids
Torch
Toilet paper
Salt
Pepper
Sauces
Cooking oil
Phone/Tablet chargers
Camera + charger

SOLUTIONS

Solutions

Solutions

Across:

2. The highest mountain on mainland Australia

4. Ayers Rock also called ____

5. The Great ____ Reef is a National icon

Down:

1. Australia is located in the ____ hemisphere

2. A ____ and an emu are on the National Emblem

3. The capital city of Australia

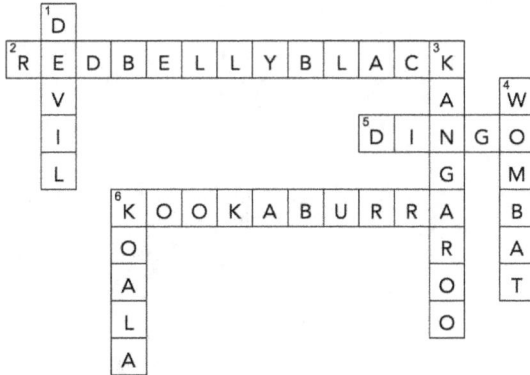

Across:

2. This snake has a coloured underside

5. Native to a Australia, but looks similar to a dog

6. Known for its entertaining 'laugh' like sound

Down:

1. Living in Tasmania, this one is little and scary-looking

3. This animal has a pouch, large feet and 'hops'

4. Round and furry and lives in a burrow

6. This animal is often mistaken for a bear

Solutions

Solutions

```
A H L T J Z D B Y B E G B Q R
K R E I C U Q C S F G A P Y K
F S N A K E D E M Z E S S P O
P Y B M P V A D L H C O D U O
L G O O L L R X K N K W C S K
A O G N F A W J Y P O A J I A
T B A T Z X H V L O I L H K B
Y U M I N A U M R S T L S B U
P Q L W L O Y A X S E A D A R
U Z S A P A G W I U A B G C R
S R G K N N S K J M F Y H E A
T U O N A V Y L L A N N C K O
T O A K O A L A J I A K E C Q
K O L V R R L Z O G H B P D F
G U X M M N W K W O M B A T R
```

KANGAROO	WALLABY	WOMBAT
POSSUM	GECKO	SNAKE
KOALA	KOOKABURRA	GOANNA
LIZARD	GALAH	PLATYPUS

```
A K O S C I U S Z K O P G A K
I S L H T W F S Y O D Y D T O
O J B R N G E A C V X E F S S
K I H M Q L B F D U K L A B C
O P N Q T K A K A D U E Y V I
P M R S R Z E J I A Z G R C U
E S O A J K D V N Y H G E U S
R P H T C U L W T F F Q S H G
A S N D B M E J R A X R R V I
H G R E A T O C E A N R O A D
O K O S B C I W E S E X C C W
U X L E P Z U D A T D B K B R
S M C R A D L E M T P A Q Y F
E O Y T H R E E S I S T E R S
N H A R B O U R B R I D G E Z
```

AYRES ROCK	THREE SISTERS	APOSTLES
OPERA HOUSE	HARBOUR BRIDGE	CRADLE MT
DESERT	KAKADU	DAINTREE
GREAT OCEAN ROAD	SHARK BAY	KOSCIUSZKO

Solutions

ACACIA   GREVILLEA   DAISIES
BANKSIA   BORONIA   MELALEUCA
WATTLE   KANGAROO PAW   WARATAH
MINT BUSH   HAKEA   EUCALYPT

WILLIAMSON   GOLD CHISEL   INXS
ACDC   BLANCHETTE   BARNES
LEDGER   CROWE   MINOGUE
KIDMAN   CROC DUNDEE   CROWDED HOUSE
MIDNIGHT OIL   DIVINYLS   YOUAMI